THE CHINA IN THE SEA

Sheila Jordan

THE AUTHOR

Sheila Gray Jordan was born in Newport, Rhode Island, and, as a Navy child, grew up in different parts of the United States. A graduate of Wellesley College, she received an M.F.A. from the Program for Writers at Warren Wilson College. She has worked for the *Kenyon Review* and directed the Ohio Poetry Circuit. She lives in Gambier, Ohio, and on a Maine island.

For my family

ACKNOWLEDGMENTS

Grateful acknowledgment is made to the following publications, in which these poems first appeared, sometimes in a different form:

Calapooya Collage, edited by Thomas Ferté: "The China in the Sea," "Mary's Halo," "Mother and Son"; the *Gambier Journal*, edited by Alexander Dashe and George Stone: "Deer Crossing"; the *Kenyon Poets*, edited by Galbraith Crump: "The Couple," "For John," "Mother Figure," "Seeing the Horses."

I wish to thank my teachers, so many of them: William Meredith, Robert Hayden, Heather McHugh, Ellen Bryant Voigt, Terry Hummer and especially Louise Glück and Ursula Le Guin.

I would also like to name William Stafford, Tillie Olsen and Pamela Painter. Counted too are those others, poets and not, who have befriended me in this life of poetry.

I thank Christopher Brookhouse, David Baker and Ann Townsend for their attentive reading and criticism.

I am grateful to Doris Jean Dilts, Martha Finan and Cy Wainscott for their help in preparing this collection.

all poems begin or end
in the garden and the sea —
— Marc Hudson

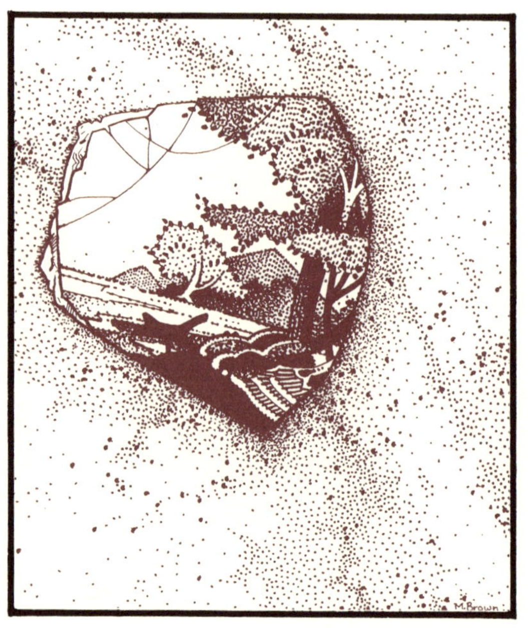
M.Brown

CONTENTS

1. I NEVER LEARNED TO SEW

MARY'S HALO

I'm stuck with it,
so that you will know me
in a crowd: Christ's mother,
the one wearing the halo.
Cimabue, Raphael, they all
painted me in it — a veil,
sometimes, flattening my hair.
It is flattering, I suppose,
off the face like the summer straws
little girls wear to church —
nothing is prettier.
My little boy wears one as well.
There is none of that tying of strings
under his chin; it simply sits
on his head.
It makes him different.
I am forever the same, "always
in style," as they say,
never going to the hatmaker's to choose
between daisies and cabbage roses, between
the velvet with the rhinestone clip
or the felt toque.
In spring, when other women's heads
turn to a new hat, I am downcast, wanting
to lift off this gold crown,
to go bareheaded.

I NEVER LEARNED TO SEW

1

The mothers of my friends
had white arms even in August.
They had small rooms at the back
of the house, or corners in bedrooms,
where the sewing machine stood,
gold-etched, glittering
like a black wasp before the window,
through which the light passed,
under the needle between their hands.

We found them there,
sewing straw into gold,
their backs turned, their thoughts
hidden like needles in haystacks.
But it was never gold
that dressed them or their children.

2

The seam between us was kept straight.
Our tongues delivered words in equal stitches,
beginning Mrs. — a buttonhole
through which we had to fit.
We did not guess their names.
Who could have guessed Pocahontas,

unless they had heard, as we did
one warm afternoon, "The Indian Love Call"
calling her? After that,
I kept her face like a penny,
bending its copper to the light
to find the Indian head — or like a miniature,
the dark braid pressed in back,
the ivory gaze maintaining
that age was not our only difference.

3

Capped sleeves, peplum, jewel neck—
the patterns came folded in envelopes,
like letters from sisters who could wear
each other's clothes.
Detailed and plain, they described lives
that stood straight and turned slowly in pins.
My child, when they held him up, was blue,
his shape all wrong side out,
reversed by his clumsy mother,
the thread misthreaded.

4

This morning, as light lines
the trees, facing them,
I think of the mothers of my friends,
the tissue paper thin beneath their fingers,

the pattern pricked out in a thousand holes.
I see the scissors cut across material,
the satin of the wedding gown fall
across their knees.

THE BOWL

1

After the fight
with my mother-in-law,
I dream the bowl is broken:
the tub of the fortieth thief;
the jar of the wine of Cana;
the milk cup.
In the dream, I cry out:
"Save yourself,"
but the bowl cracks
in the firing,
the fault
nicking through.

2

A seagull builds a castle
in the air, hangs
to drop a mussel, a crab
down onto the rocks.
The shell snaps open,
and the body is unearthed.
The water is a bowl
patterned with the bodies
of my children,
who fish with their hands

on the bottom of Chandler's Cove
for the shard of blue.

3

From the pieces, from the wet hands
of my husband, his brother,
our sons and the nephew cousins—
deep divers, good swimmers—
my father-in-law has reassembled it.
Raised, intact, except for
one fragment, the bowl stands in his study.
Blue and white,
crazed, it is as old
as Crete, as water.
It will never be filled.

"A BLACKBIRD, HENRY"

> *Come on with me, come on with me,*
> *Milandy Lee, and let us sing*
> *this melody.*

"Look who's beautiful!"
A whistle scoots down the back
of her neck, between
her shoulder blades, going
right on doing
those things, so that
she turns her head.

Turns it back: "Huh."
She lifts her chin and continues
down the walk between the enlisted men's barracks,
a no man's land for women — for a girl
who goes there to get
to the officers' quarters.

She lives here.
To drive onto the Navy Base,
her mother stops at the guard post,
gives her husband's name and rank.
The girl faces front in the Packard,
at ease when the sailor makes
his half-salute.

From the parade ground,
"The Stars and Stripes Forever,"
moves her to swing out.
"Hey, honey!"
Again, a whistle, a wolf call —
a shadow, shadows — so
she watches her step.
By the brig, a chorus starts,
as if rising from a cage of singing birds,
birds that hang on the window bars.

"You can be put in the brig
for chasing an officer's daughter."
But they are in the brig.
And she listens to the notes
flutter and drop.

At bedtime, when she was small,
she would ask her father for the song
with speaking parts:
    "You sing just like a bird."
    "What kind of bird, Milandy Lee?"
    "A blackbird, Henry!"
They laughed over that bird,
navy blue in the sunlight,

black in the night
and without wing bars.

SEEING THE HORSES

When my son wakes, I say,
"We will go to see the horses."
In my head I see them.
Nightly, I exercise them for him,
singing: *Black and bay,*
dapple and gray. Coach and six-a
little horses.

At breakfast, I hear the clopping feet, the cry:
clop, "Rags," clop, "Vegetables." "Get up!"
Trot, trot over the bridge.
The sun burns hot on the garden,
and my son, in his pajamas,
drenches his Rice Krispies in milk.
"Let's go to see the horses," I say.

In my mind they are far off,
though they can get no further
than the bottom of the pasture.
We walk beside the fence,
until I spot the chestnut and brown
in their velvet investiture,
in Queen Anne's lace, down by the pond.
"Tiger. Jack," the boy shouts,
as mounting the rails, we drop
into the field.
Looking the other way and the other,
the two rangy geldings amble up.

Close to, they are no vision:
burrs in their coats and tails,
fetlocks caked with mud.
Quiet, all the same, I see
Jack stands big above the child.
Fingers flat, holding out palms,
we treat them with apples and sugar.
The boy reaches further, trying his hand
on shoulder, barrel, and flank,
as Jack throws his head—
widens an eye.
Now my son embraces the neck,
grabs after the withers and mane—
as if, were I to give him a leg up
onto the bare back, to ride.

OLD MAID

1

Not enough to play Michigan,
we two divide the table,
keeping our usual places— making it one sided.
This June the youngest child and I
occupy the five-bedroom summer house.
It feels like it did that first summer
without the children.
I do not step immediately into a room
but stop in a doorway and look
to see if the furniture can be rearranged,
a vase perhaps moved on the mantel.

2

For our first child, the spinster
whose island house it was
gave us a pink blanket.
He slept in a room papered with rosebuds,
as did the other boys.
It was all here: birthday cards, four-leaf
clovers in the dictionary and games
without directions, except
the many pieces spelling time.
A wooden box holds papers inked
in oriental characters, wrapping

ivory sticks, dotted like dominoes.
Unintelligible, they are like footprints
that stop in snow — moves
I cannot follow.

3

The boy and I play Old Maid.
Ugly, a stock character,
she stands up in my hand.
As a girl, I hated her so much
I tore the card in two.
My son pairs policemen, cowboys,
and Indians — as if one could find a life
like one's own and choose it.
Soon he will go out,
and I shall be left with the Old Maid.
Already the other boys are out.
Like a wild card, my husband comes and goes.

4

"Time for bed," I tell him.
The boy takes himself upstairs,
and I pick up the cards,
undoing the neat duplications
that lie across the table.
The Old Maid I face down,
feeling her place — not distributed —
at the center of the deck.

Rising, I see the spinster's books
side by side with mine, her watercolor
of the shore, so dimly amateur
it might have been done by either of us.

5

A crossover connects the bedroom
and the upper barn, where
her papier-mâché and wicker dress form
is stored, back against the wall—
a wall flower.
Attached to it, like a dance card,
hangs a luggage tag with the name:
Miss Florence Dulaney.
Who would wish to change it?
Unclaimed, hourglass correct,
it is a fine figure of a woman.

THE ARK

The child is stubborn.
She wants *her* way,
not the one
that comes with the box
of toy animals.
Clearly the sun is out:
it shines on the yellow cabin,
on the orange sunroof that opens
to let in the good weather and passengers.
Even the underside is dyed sun red,
tattooed: *Made in Mexico.*
It is a pleasure boat.
The adults bend down,
but not by their procedure
will she herd the animals.
In random numbers they browse the rug:
three are friends; two are sisters.
On board, a giraffe waves to a giraffe—
not a traveler.
Those that ride take turns.
Sometimes when she cannot tell
which went last, two go together.
In this way they continue,
until it is time to take her bath.
All the animals get on board.
Animals from other boxes ship too.
What happens is the ark sinks.
Together they float to the surface.
One by one she saves them.

BRER RABBIT AND THE TAR BABY

> *A good story compels you like*
> *sexual hunger but the pace is more leisurely.*
> *And there are always melons.*
>
> — *Robert Hass*

The briers, with their thorns
like hoodwinking stars, told the story,
about which her mother,
who did not tell stories, said:
"It's no bed of roses."
In the middle of the brier patch,
the rabbit undergoes a transformation:
it becomes a girl, her ankles crossed,
her elbows on her knees, chin in her hands.
She is called back to herself
by the final twist, the risible crow:
"I was born and bred in a brier patch!"
When she teases, "Daddy, tell me a story,"
he seems to consider and then begins:
"Did you ever hear the story of Brer Rabbit
and the Tar Baby?"
"Don't you know any other story?" she sighs.
At the wedding, walking down the aisle,
he commenced it. . . .
The Tar Baby, that empress it was whose melons
they thumped, whose victory she nearly snatched

from the hubris — only to have it go skipping off.
"That Brer Rabbit!" Troubadour, wily talker of words,
he had "cotched" her.
In the story there was no telling
of the flight: the upswing, the sun in the pines,
the free fall. . . . Her father would draw out:
"But *please* don't throw me in the brier patch!"
until its target was her one desire, and,
despite herself, she pitches in.

MR. JAMES

A girl-child had better keep out
of a horse barn, away
from livery stables.
That is why I went.
He had a mouth like a mule—
brown, tobacco-edged— the mules
I wouldn't feed carrots,
saving them for the infrequent
horse or pony he took in trade.

I didn't get to ride—
not even to sit on a back.
But one afternoon,
he beckoned me into his office.
He lifted me up, like a princess,
onto a high stool.
When his hand came between my pants
and my body, I tried to smile,
to smooth my dress.

"Whoa there, whoa there, girlie,"
he told me,
his hand working up
under me, fingernailed, prizing—
as if to fasten
a cinch.
Long as church or dinner I sat,

wanting to be excused, to get down.
When Mr. James turned me out the door,
he swatted my backside,
like he did the mules',
to get going.

I did, and I never told,
repeating my silence
like a fire I set, like the red mule
that when he jerked the halter
would not halt, but
went up and up.

2. WOMEN WALKING

WOMEN WALKING

> *In the nineteenth century*
> *"one of the careers open to*
> *women was perpetual childhood."*
> — *Richard Chase*

"Ready?" they call.
"Ready," she answers,
the paragraph cut short.

They assemble in the hall
in tight-nipped jackets and heavy skirts,
ready for the walk. The doors open,
and they step quickly through,
turning up their faces to the sky.
The weather ties its ribbons
under their chins. They link waists
down the steps, on down the gravel drive.

From a distance I watch;
I care for them.
Miles they trudged, as if the paths
between the houses of their acquaintance
were deep forest reaching to land's end.
One step down, a woman of the streets.
One step up, a life above reproach.
What did and did not happen?

He waits, ready in the road,
his hat lifted to greet them.
The novels close, but walking, walking,
the women come out inside themselves.

"BYE, BABY BUNTING"

The old stories linger,
we know them by heart: the infant
on the doorstep and the lopsided,
miscreant mother, a figure
hurrying away.

Mother sang on the side
of my bed her nightly songs
to lull me to sleep,
and I was comfortable, unless
I heeded the words:

"The bees and the butterflies,
Buzzing round its eyes,
The poor little thing
Cried Mammy." Or the rape,
in which a rabbit's skin

was skinned, loosed
by a trick of hunting,
by the significant Daddy, who fetched it
". . . to wrap his Baby Bunting in."
I would fall asleep.

The dream (it was the under-
belly I turned up
when I shut my eyes), time

25

and again I dreamed it,
along with daydreams

and novels, fourteen
and reaching down: *My Antonia* . . .
Nana — any book with a girl's name.
"Mother," the dream begins.
I face her, my arms outstretched.

"Mother," but the story unfolds,
and I am carrying a bundle —
a subject. Snow falls, whiting out
the lone hill farm, the rutted road,
my mother's form.

I look down into the face.
My hands enter the snow's silk purse
to dig it under,
the pig-child, nearby a tree
I mark, deeply mantled.

THE MAN WHO LIKES COWS

Thirty miles from the city,
past the first town
with a small name,
cows are in a field,
black and white Holsteins,
nudes with dairy nipples.

He stops the car,
opens the door on my side,
and I get out to see the cows
who look at us over their shoulders—
sloppy, dumb broads, wading
in milk and honeybees.

He is a man who likes cows.
But they are not to be coaxed,
cud-happy this spring day,
the grass green.
Something big—a bell or a sunset—
is necessary to move them.

Like Jove, "Speaking
their tongue . . . ," in his city suit,
he cups his hands: the *Moo*
rising from his groin,
a brazen klaxon,
helloing.

The call bends their thick skulls.
They lift their heads —
all eyes and ears —
coming on to crowd the fence.
I take his hand, make a fist of it
with its gold ring.

MOTHER'S COOKING

To understand this, you've got to understand
how it was between us—
that extended family each summer.
In the morning, the phone would ring,
and it would be my mother calling
about what to have for dinner.

Lying in bed, only just waking
beside my husband to the birds, to the day,
I would hear the apples' heavy thump,
Mother picking the Golden Transparents.
Kneeling at the upstairs window,
I would see her in the wet raspberries,
gathering — as if we were a primitive tribe.

Unless it was Saturday, cartoon day,
the children couldn't wait
for my limp slices of French toast—
the orange juice *sour*. They'd swallow
a Flintstone vitamin, a half-glass of milk
and be out the door to her kitchen
for applesauce and sticky buns.

I'd have a second cup of coffee
on the front steps, our make-do deck,
dress, and walk over to the other house
to find it neat as a pin, Mother and the boys

gone fishing on her note under the plate
of tollhouse cookies. I'd eat one,
take one to my father in his garden.
From the chimney, Mother's gull,
its carton of scraps beside the sink,
would cry down to us. My father
would pull an onion, drop a potato bug
into a bottle of kerosene, we two looking
over the garden: doing well, corn tasseling.

"String beans or squash?" I didn't care,
but I'd answer one or the other,
and she would cook them both.
Big meals.
After dinner she washed, I dried.
The drain emptied, stove wiped, we'd walk
to the Point to see the sunset.

Last night we arrived on the island.
Mother cooked lobsters,
French fries and lemon meringue pie,
as usual. This morning she hasn't called.
I wait, finally call her.
The telephone rings nine times
before she picks it up. (My father died
in the winter. Some days she sleeps
a little later, she's said.)

"What shall we have for dinner?" I ask her.
She doesn't answer, until I almost think
she hasn't heard me.
"It's your family," she says — without
emphasis — and my stomach goes empty.

TWO TEMPERATURES

When her son came home,
he had flunked the test.
She could have told him
there would be a question
on the difference between Celsius
and Fahrenheit, that the teacher
would expect him to be able to convert
one to the other.
She could have got out the dictionary
and found the two temperatures,
the drawing of the thermometer
with the Centigrade and Fahrenheit scales,
their slippery mercuries
two sides of an equation.

What she herself remembers is perhaps
like what he had in mind
taking the test: icicle downspouts
on the porch, the kettle steaming.
There was an outdoor thermometer with
a snowman blowing frosty breath at zero,
a robin singing at sixty-five.
There were sun and shadow on a blue fence—
all of which made a difference,
like the words in the story problems
that took her attention,
so she wanted not to factor or reduce,

but to ride in the red automobile from
Trenton to Cape May.

She learned. She learned
not to look up until she had the answer.
And later she learned to love a man so hot
on her cool skin, she threw
the covers off.
She thinks of this, and flashes—
hot and cold — go through her,
her hand on the boy's shoulder,
where he sits fiddling fork
and spoon together.

GRETCHEN

> *What more is there to love*
> *than I have loved?*
> > — *Wallace Stevens*

1

The poet answers, *enough.*
I have loved enough.
She decides to go back to her garden,
to her husband, and to her four sons.

Stacking her poetry in a cardboard box,
she packs it up. The poems
fit down, as if for the first time
bound in a book — a sizable book,

the kind with soft, ruffled pages,
fingered and read.
It is good, she thinks. And she feels good—
almost can take her word.

2

In the garden the first morning,
she smiles. Gardening,
she digs around her feet, gardener
and poet in one easy posture,

setting out the nursery plants.
The poet cannot let go of the watering can;
stepping carefully down the rows,
she lowers and lifts the light rain.

Weary, the gardener stacks the flats,
gathers up the tools, and pauses
at the edge of the garden, where poet
and gardener alike admire the work.

3

The house stands a few steps from the garden.
She walks to it, thinking
of her son and the operation
he must have — how she must try to love it.

In the kitchen, she makes lunch,
using store lettuce and tomatoes,
telling herself she will soon have her own.
Salt and pepper, mustard . . .

she puts the food on the table,
calling for them to come and eat.
One gesture, pouring a milk —
no more than a line break — brings him,

the one not as quick,
to the table with the rest.

DEER CROSSING

1

I take a deep breath.
We begin to climb the hills
godsending two good-size mountains
above the interstate.

A deer rears on a crossing sign.

I look for it in the camouflage
of forest and small clearings
between the miles, to where
we pass a car on the shoulder,
a man getting out.

"What's that?" you ask.

Before I can stop my eyes,
I see the deer. I think it is a horse
rolling and kicking.

2

On Bishop's Backbone, the deer
turn toward the highway.
It is first light.
The woods are open, without leaves

nearly treeless, and the deer
leap clean as Xs. Gun season.
I slow the car.
One hangs back—I motion
it to cross.

3

Singing: *Over the river*
and through the woods . . . ,
coming back from the airport with our son
in late November,
we see the deer.
Like the three fingers he held up
when he was three,
they are like the three of us.

4

I take a blanket from the bed
and go out into the field
where the deer stood.
Except, perhaps, to have circled,
it hasn't moved.

Head low, it is on its feet
under the tree that names
the farm: Sugartree.
It is 3:00 a.m.
I fold my arms in the blanket

and walk close —
too close for comfort?

The white tail does not show,
and though the blanket slips off
my shoulders, I keep my hands closed,
crossed on the fringe,
not to smooth over the darkness
between us.

3. THE GIFT

THE GIFT

1

It is Christmas
as this story begins.
The shops, the night, the necessity
are familiar.
I say to you:
"We are like O. Henry's characters
Della and Jim
in 'The Gift of the Magi.' "

The gift we seek
is for our son. From store
to store, we walk the mall
in the confusion of the holiday season.
Hesitating, not a man of words,
but correctly, the surgeon
used "salvage"
to describe the operation.

2

In the nursery school parking lot,
where the four-year-old and I get out,
a mother and child hurry up
to ask about the new baby.
"We lost him," I reply.

At which the child — amazed —
responds:
"How could you do that?"

3

The box is in the window
of the gift shop.
Flowered like a Swiss child's
vest or skirt, it is pine.
We point to it.
Smiling, the shopgirl lifts it out

and winds it for us,
a music box to contain
the ashes of our son. The song it plays,
"Somewhere, My Love," is the song
I sang — not meaning it —
a lullaby.

LITTLE SISTER

Her mother shuts the door.
The little sister grips
the handle of the doll carriage.
She is a "big girl."
Each day, waiting for the baby,
they encourage her to grow bigger.
She shakes the carriage.
"You are a baby," she tells the doll,
although she knows it is not a baby—
that she must imagine it—
tucking in the covers.

She knows her mother doesn't imagine.
And she guesses her father doesn't,
rolling up the evening paper and
slapping it against his leg
as he nods to her:
"The stork is on the way."
Jerking the baby buggy hard,
so the doll falls on its face,
she says it over:
"The stork is on the way!"
"The stork is on the way!"

Head down, arms pushing,
she spins the carriage so fast
the wheels lift off the ground.

Like the ocean, the sky is blue and empty,
but soon a wave will come,
a white crest will break into a bird.
Wings beating, the stork will drop to the feeder,
where her mother scatters corn.

The child hugs herself.
She will have the baby.
She reaches inside her pocket— yes.
Snapping open its bill, laying down
the knotted napkin, the stork
will eat the goldfish.

PRAYER

I was taught to pray.
And since I had got it into my head
that prayer was sexual, that
Mary and the Angel — their hands
clasped upward — prayed
the baby Jesus, I prayed.

"Who made you?"
"God made me," and I understood,
therefore, that I was His choice
to be female. I complained.
The miracle I suggested was not great —
small, really — if He would hear me.

Only in that way could I have
my mother's best love,
my father's uncompromising pride,
the world's first chances.
"Dear God," I urged,
"make me a boy."

I did not pray in bed.
On cold nights, I knelt naked
at the open window.
"Lord of Hosts. . . ."
"Almighty God our Father," I spoke out loud,
loading my words, trying to lift them up
into the night sky.

Like a knife my body
slid beneath the sheets,
my thighs compressing my cold hands,
locked together for warmth,
after my "Amen."

FOR JOHN

1 Speaking of the Dead

Why do we keep our dead
secret? The *you*
we address, the star
in the window.

The word in my mouth
is one syllable. Under my tongue
I hold it with words
of one syllable.

It is easy to lose:
one day laughing, I nearly
swallowed it; talking to a stranger,
I almost spit it out.

If being careful not to speak
can keep our dead in health,
we will not speak.
I didn't,

though under my tongue
was growing a second tongue
I couldn't bite
that *would* speak.

2 Sick Child

The child is sick.
Night stops.

The house, like a body
locating pain, refuses it,
holds still.
I turn out of bed,
out of a sound night's sleep:
untroubled, quietly breathing
in my flannel nightdress.

The child whimpers.
He has kicked off the covers.
Worry lifts a hot hand;
my sleeves hang.

On the wall the night light
flattens. On the pillow
day can hardly raise
its head.

3 My Death

> *That did not die two deaths*
> *as mothers do. . . .*
> — *Michael Hamburger*

My death is finished —
one. After this first,
I am not immune,
but continue out of quarantine
to guard my health,
this afterlife,
with the prescription
mothers keep
out of the children's reach:
that a next not catch sick;
that the death is my own
and no other.

4 The Rattle

The mother examines the rattle.
A fear she has —
along with the Teddy bear's glass eyes —
is that the rattle will break,
its thin plastic crack
in the child's mouth, releasing
the babble, discharging a pellet
in the child's throat.
She consigns the rattle
to the dangerous collection
she makes: blue, yellow and white,
putting them carefully aside.
Unlooked-for, God, come round
like an offhand great uncle,
welcome in the nursery,
chucks the child under the chin,
winks — jangling his brass keys
and uttering nonsense.

5 For John

November 14-December 2

The solid child
behind the spoon
is not you.
Words I feed you,
your first solids,
wanting to make you plump,
to put the silver spoon in your mouth.
Like a Chinese parent,
I chew each bite,
preparing the food,
gingerly suspending it
between us — my mouth open.
The ache relaxes, and my breasts
are empty.
"Child," I croon,
"open your mouth."
With words I feed you.

6 Feeding the Stars

At dawn, what can I place
on the windowsill?
All night they have hungered,
the stars in their rooms.
Now it is time to feed them.
What can I place on the windowsill?
A crumb?
They are tired of crumbs?
The stars desire to be seated
above the salt, places of honor
at the banquet table.
Not like us — not visionary —
they do not want our wishes.
What will you feed us?
is what they always ask.

4. LOOKING BACK

LOOKING BACK

Every morning she circles
the pond. For a long
time she is alone.
Then one morning there
is a child with her.

She continues to circle the pond,
and in the next few years
there is another child.
One year, though surely
she is pregnant — see how she walks —
there is no new child.

Squatting, dipping in sticks,
the children teach her
about the pond.
Ducks, bottomless, swim Vs,
and turtles pedal off the logs.
In winter she stands on the ice,
watching the children skate.
One day she holds out her arms
and walks clear across.

On the opposite side,
she turns and looks back.
In the center is the big rock
the pond exposes. Above,

marked by a paint slash,
under leaf pulp and down branches,
the path goes on.

One day and the next,
she doesn't come. When she does,
she stands looking across
the pond's surface, in which
are trees and a landscape full of water—
a cloud, tipped like a paper cup,
filling, draining.

THE CHEEK

> *the women talk,*
> *their cheeks gleam like diamonds. . . .*
> — *Beatrice Hawley*

It was difficult for the daughter to know
which cheek her mother turned,
which she hid.
A full face smiled back.

If there was a shadow, it was near
the eyes. Arms touching,
they polished Romans for the centerpiece,
the red cheeks of the apples brightening,
a green shiner coming up
under the dish towel.

The girl watched over her Jane Austen.
When her father leaned to kiss her mother,
she would turn her cheek,
and the daughter guessed which:
the hurt one to be made better,
or a fresh wound?

Flowers never dropped in the house
or in the garden. Her mother's
quick fingers picked off

the brown heads. A trickle of bleach
kept the water in the vases clear.

At the funeral Mass, the priest
kisses the word. Her mother's
powdered cheeks are patches the daughter
wants to wipe
with her wet handkerchief.
It is balled in her lap with the Bible,

loose spined, black ribboned,
pummeled, as if
by a fist. Soft
as a cheek under her hand.

MOTHER FIGURE

Inside the mother is the girl.
The neighbor boy has teased her;
the children have sent her to her room.
Inside the mother, she can't get out;
the children are watching.
If she will pretend to be the mother
in her hip-length sweater,
the children will look away.
If she behaves herself—
stands in the door and waves—
they will say goodbye.
A tower of boxes in her arms,
she climbs the attic stairs,
from which to descend,
she must grow into that old woman
with the humped back.

CAPTIVE . . . RED PONEY

A painting by Martin Garhart

Over the desk is the watercolor of the horse.
Some days it is too much for her,
and she imagines turning its mirror
to the wall. What began by liking,
by encouraging the work of a friend,
what began as seeing color and form—
though these continue to flourish—
what began as a safe hazard, buying a picture,
gets down to the artist: she reading
and the picture speaking to her.

It speaks in a fragment from an early draft:
the messenger . . . stars in his crown . . .
in haste and zeal arrives,
and the horse, wet, flanks heaving,
is released:
    into the fields
    of the unspared horses,
lines she had shut in a drawer,
not finding a place until here.

She raises her eyes to the picture of the horse,
red, shading to pink, to white, to paper,
and to the unclothed woman on its back,
her hands bound behind her.

As the woman looks or does not look,
she looks: space like a vista or a bandage.
She guesses — the lower face awash —
at the mouth, open or closed,
at a lead rope, dropped by the Dakota artist —
at the half-clad Indian off the page,
the tent, the narrative.

She thinks, as a rider about to fall thinks:
I am falling. But does not fall yet,
the horse solid under her, its regular,
irregular motion meeting her body.
"Drop your reins," the riding instructor calls.
"Sit down, sit down," as the canter extends.
And, incredibly: "Hold out your hands,"
as the jump approaches.

Yes, she is falling, loose
as water over rock, under the hooves,
straddling the question of the gallop:
Can the four feet leave the ground all together?
Red pony, spotted ponies, black and white,
the hooves pass over her, the horses
raising a cloud of dust — a plume —
out of which furlong a red pony,
riderless, continues to run.

THE COUPLE

Two figures sit before the fire.
She looks to the side, checking,
making her insignificant comparison.
An old man and an old woman,
together they gaze into the fire,
its matched flames, its vivid colors.
She looks again, and he is further
by a whisker from the blaze.

In the coarse adjustment of their ages—
she the younger from the start—
when did his advantage slip
and she begin to get the better?
She smoothes her needlepoint,
the green leaves, and considers
the story of Baucis and Philemon,
the perfect couple, whose wish

to die together was at first
hers, the wife's idea.
The bright visitors are gone,
and she can change her mind.
Half-ready, half-not, she lifts a log
onto the fire, bending to poke it,
to watch the smoke eddy,
the flame flicker and catch.

She looks up. In his green robe
and arctic slippers, the man
beside her settles back. When
will the metamorphosis occur? Unraveling
the emerald wool from her basket, she rethreads
her needle, searches a stem between
the many leaves and stitches. For some time
he has said no word.

VOWS

"She'll fool you,"
he'd say, about the hind foot,
the river,
the boat, and,
by implication, them—
women. All this
without malice.

Side-stepping, holding fast
to the gunnels,
she awaited his second, unburdening
"Amen" to the minister's
sea of troubles.
And when she met "her companion,"
her father's ironic name for himself,
she gave her "I do,"
taking also her mother's blessing:

"You can say anything if you smile."

READING THE CARDS

I come back to the three-year-old
on her father's shoulders.
I remember her. I remember
being up there on my father's shoulders.

The flocked pine cone tree, unpacked
from the cardboard box, marked
Pine Cone Christmas Tree,
stands on the red felt runner

in the center of the dining table,
awash with cards. "Imagine,"
I speak aloud: "Jack, a father,"
and pass the card to you. *At Squam, '93,*

for George's 60th, it reads.
You are sixty, and we had a small party
for you in June. The lake, ironed
like a best tablecloth, is spread out

behind the family, and she is wearing
a bathing suit, looking incomprehensibly
toward Christmas. I remember
my father's hands anchoring my feet—

that high-altitude doubleness—
being able to look down on my brother,

pulled up on my mother's knees.
Jack smiles into the camera.

His daughter's hands grip his head.
I remember that transcendence, Athena
springing from the brow of Zeus.
Like George, half-smiling, slumped,

you return the card to me,
you, whose head I still can turn,
having learned early and taught the family,
how to make a man run, jump.

BEGGARS' NIGHT

Year by year, Halloween is draining.
The trees empty into the sky, their leaves,
like weights, dropping the scale

down, lifting a bare pan.
We turn off the light, leaving the porch
dark, the odd tooth in the jack-o-lantern's

glowing smile, street talk in the village
for no trick or treat at this house.
And halfway, we are sorry.

We are the ghosts behind the glass,
the hunched crazies in the hall.
But the cupboard is bare.

We've not even a bag of apples.
To get away, we drive to Loudonville
to the Brass Plate. On Route 3,

it is rural Ohio night: the dark
siding of woods and barns; the "nowhere
special" from which we come—

and "going nowhere" either.
The front tables in the restaurant
are box seats on the Halloween parade.

In back, wearing out-of-town faces,
we look over ribs and coleslaw,
the candle's rustic orange. *Gossamer,*

I whisper, touching my lips
to the word, wanting to finger
the costume of the child, dressed

as a fairy princess, star wanded.
Her father — I assume — drinks a beer,
talks with the woman behind the bar.

We pay, take pieces of candy corn.
Doors dark, houses show back-lit.
Marsupial, ghostly slow, an opossum

crosses the highway — glare blind
on the center line. I look back.
There are no lights after ours.

5. HEAVEN AND EARTH

HEAVEN AND EARTH

We have ascended into the attic and made it real.
We have walked off the center and given it legroom.
Like the family trip to Yosemite that summer,
we have arrived to pitch a tent.
Not all the forest floor, not all the attic,
not all the house from which the furniture
was carried is included, but enough
to pack a mid-size U-Haul van.

With room enough for the living room
and scattered other pieces:
the hall mirror, a child's chair, miscellaneous
boxes of china, toss pillows, blankets.
You name it. Help me to sort it out.

We say we are saving it for the children,
whose lives, unrolling the Hamadan,
embracing a stranger on its blue field,
we can scarcely imagine.
"In keeping," your mother would have said

of the stripe and the floral, your head
against the one, mine the other—
arms resting on the chair arms.
Who are we? Ghosts?

Children, ducked under a velvet rope,
cordoning off the space?
You the Daddy, I the Mommy.
Look. How well it fits:
the wing chair and the club face to face;
her cupboard out from the wall;
no curtains — a sheet hung against
the fading dormer light.

"Easy does it, easy does it."
Between you and the neighbor boy,
you lower the couch.
Your chest heaves, having moved heaven and earth
to get the thing up two flights of stairs.
I follow with the cushions.
"Here we are," you announce, as you used to,
pulling in the drive.
And we'd climb out of the station wagon,
cross the dark lawn — the children lagging —
into that house, someone brushing the rocker.

SALT AND PEPPER

After grace, his next words
would be, "Pass
the salt and pepper,"
never the one without the other,
though a guest at his table,
a stranger to this courtesy, might ask
for salt *or* pepper.
And we would pass them both.
The Morton Salt walked
its girl with her umbrella
through the rain in the kitchen,
under her arm a box
pouring salt: *when it rains*
it pours — a negligence
or lesson, I could not be sure.
Mother measured a pinch
in the palm of her hand.
Still he lifted the wide-holed shaker,
salting the salty dinner,
not adding pepper. "Unhealthy,"
she warned.
At the funeral, she places a rose.
We cup our handfuls of dirt.
It falls on his coffin
like too much pepper.

THE BED

Nights, knowing full well
where it was, making
her way from the bathroom, how often
did she bump into his bed, jogging him
awake to her.
Nights now, she is tempted
to move to it, the sheets clean
and cold — how often
should she change them?

Ought she to take out the bed?
It is a question
the widow asks herself,
rising from the other,
her energy high, the day bright,
her mind clear.
Strict in her arrangements —
a place for everything —
she has made a clean sweep.

She looks at it.
What will she do?
Last spring she bought
new springs and mattresses.
What is done?
What are the means by which
one survives the other?

She can't think
of the room without it,
strewn with her nightdress.

Smoothing the spread, cool,
dispassionate, her hand
slips beneath the pillow, exploring
another world.

MOTHER AND SON

Our weight is nearly equal in the boat.
He drives it, and I sit facing forward.
The oars, the fishing poles and tackle box,
the extra gas he has stowed down the sides,
so that the way is clear. For me,
I have only the paunchy lunch bag in my lap
and my straw hat — a mistake — that I anchor
with one hand, the other on the gunnel.
The path between the islands is plain,
plain on water as it is not from land,
where islands appear to overlie one another
like harbor seals basking, colonizing
ledges raised by the tide.
A good day for me to go out, I have only
to let the boat, let my son take me,
the fog lifting, boats on their moorings
not finding a wind, the current steering.
"Glass water," he tells me.
I try to sit in the middle, be ready,
as he opens her up, and the bow tilts high.
Spray wets the seat. My hat folds back.
What do I know about boats?
I know my son. I try not to worry.
He adjusts the speed a notch, water worsening
like river rapids. Something, he shouts,
and I look to where his waving arm points.
I see water. I bend to see under the water.

It is he who first spots the sunken log drifting
and turns the boat away.
He cuts the motor. Here is the fishing ground.
I look back. We are a distance from land.
My son attaches a jig, unlocks the reel
and casts my line. The mackerel are running big:
"horse mackerel," he calls them.
The pole bows to the fish I bring flashing in.
My son nets it. I watch as he removes the hook.
Ask to throw it back. My son looks at me.
He lifts the heavy fish overboard.
Not letting go, he strokes it through the water,
back and forth, back and forth, feathering its gills
until it jackknifes on oxygen
and swims down.

BLUE SKY

Cloudless. You sleeping the sleep
of a young man.
I go down the stairs in
bare feet, not to disturb you,
having this new consideration
of your independence, and
what I do not know about last night.

Last night,

you put on an Allman Brothers tape
for my tin ears, tuned to PBS
for cooking dinner,
to *South Pacific*, the Andrews Sisters— eons
before you,
hat backwards, straddling
a kitchen chair.

At times like this, I feel
what it is to have had you late.
I ask the name of the music,
and you tell me:
"Blue Sky." Adding:
"I'd think you would know it,
knowing me."

Between us, this is an outpouring.
I smile:
"Blue skies, smiling at me, nothing
but blue skies. . . ."

Blue to the ocean, blue
to the bay. A gull crosses
white against blue.
This morning we're out of milk.
Your truck's behind me in the drive.
I take your keys.

On the seat, I read:
        "Let's make love."
                Blue Sky

Private, not your writing,
blue ballpoint on blue lines,
the writing knows you.
I turn the key. The stereo blasts.
I sing along, the truck
backing in the ruts, easy
rolling out.

THE BOAT TO CLIFF

Out here we get on without
buying a ticket.
And we will come back
on the afternoon trip.
    It is of importance because
we are crossing water.

Three times I have phoned
the Portland office, outwaiting
the recording to speak in person,
to be assured
    that the boat will return us.
Because of my mother.

She is eighty-seven, and we will
be on foot among
the day-trip bicyclers.
The young deck hand takes
    her elbow. Her other arm
carries her folded white sweater

and purse — squat and necessary
as a sea chest. Already
Gene backs up the Ford pickup
with the mail, the hawsers unloop,
    the lines fall away.
"Free as a bird," she says,

taking a seat. Free?
I ask myself if I should ask
about the tickets, if
we shouldn't have two stubs
     like those — like feathers
in the hatband of the man whose

camcorder pans the island,
our details picked out
against the background evergreen:
Sanford's Beach, the Nubbles—
     a wade at low tide.
"Anchors aweigh . . . ," my mother hums,

"Anchors aweigh."
The tune flutters like a streamer
from a sailing, like a line
thrown to my father in the Pacific
     during World War II.
Cool on the water, the breeze

is just cool enough for her sweater
on the boat to Cliff,
the last island after ours
on the Bay Tour, a short segment
     of blue hyphens
before the *Island Holiday* docks.

On the wharf: the same black Lab,
two kids fishing mackerel.

Mother greets a woman of no age
in a Fair Isle knit:
    "Do I know her?"
I check my watch.

The road circles the island,
wooded, fir inside of fir,
like Russian dolls.
Turn-of-the-century cottages.
    Bicycles and golf carts
that pass for cars

pass us, the occupants waving,
slowing, it seems,
for Mother, who waves back,
sunlight on her side.
    "A heavenly day. Heavenly,"
she calls it, boarding the boat.

LITTLE AUNT RULIE

It's her chair —
little Aunt Rulie's,
a child's chair, empty,
with a jar of ferns in water
set before it in the family picture.

The family is gathered around
in a family way, dutiful to the mother's
wish, at whose instance the chair is lifted
and placed out on the lawn with them,
where, off her lap, under her hand,

the youngest child would kneel.
Grown up into second and third rows,
the children hoist their own children,
kin and in-law every other, little Aunt Rulie's
tribe, she at the source, akin to the earth

mother, the aunt they tell or do not
tell about: run-off, disappeared, taken
as it were, until each comes to understand
death. Pushed forward at Grandmother's behest,
dressed in her best invisible presence,

little Aunt Rulie sits tight in her chair,
child-aunt, claimant, claimed.

THE CHINA IN THE SEA

1

"Not for all the tea in China,"
the words come out — not a straight "No,"
and I wonder what it was
that prompted me to say them?
You say the house is haunted.
So is the beach.

Willowware? Staffordshire?
When I walk, patterns turn up
in the sand. The edges are flowered,
embroidered like a piece of cross-stitch
spelling, "Home, Sweet Home."
The green and white leaf and key—
so-called Hamilton Hotel service—
is from the inn that stood above the beach
and burned in the 1930s.

Did it all fall into the sea?
From what pre-paper-plate picnics,
washed away, did it come?

2

Ironstone, Crown Derby, Doulton.
I imagine the women throwing the china;

I see them on the beach, as the men get off
in their boats. Arming themselves,
the women hurl their Haviland, serving up
soup bowls and dinner plates—
breaking the sets—while
astern, the men drop over bottles
that tilt and drift back.

3

I pick up the pieces.
The glass is like rain—like water
over the dam—crystal falling. But the china
is different. Wanting a whole cup, a saucer,
I collect it, as they, in a like mood,
must have swept up.

The sun sets, and the window ledges
of the house are littered
with china and glass that catch
the light and hold my eyes.
I lay two plates and set the glasses.
Foot in the door, you call me
to open it for you, fanning out
two lobsters, which, stiff-armed
as a fishwife, I take.

THE LILAC ROOM

I find the pattern in the pattern book.
Why do I want to cover these walls..
with lilacs, when they bloom
just outside?
This is a small house,
unchanging, except
as light changes
and in where we sit.
There is no room for this intrusion,
lilacs dripped from the brush,
great gorgeous bouquets,
heart swollen and purple. This room
fits a bed and a bureau,
a straight chair and throw rug.
Still, I apply the paste,
drop the paper,
and the strips unroll
like a curtain going up
on an empyrean scene: cloudy,
overstuffed, unlikely
inside as sky or water —
into which I enter.
Flowering overhead,
the lilacs are everywhere.
In armfuls, about my ankles,
they breathe.
Increasingly, we breathe together.